CONTENTS

GW01007160

WONDERS OF THE WORLD

The earth, sea and air are full of wonderful creatures. Today we can read all about them and look at them in films or photos. Long ago, reports went round by word of mouth, and no one was sure what to believe. Here are some stories of four creatures that may exist – or may not!

The Kraken

The Kraken is an enormous creature living deep in the sea. For months on end it sleeps on the seabed. Then on hot summer days, when the sea is calm, it rises slowly to the surface. That is when it does terrible harm to sailors: it pulls their ships down under the water in the huge whirlpool it makes when it goes back home.

About the Beast

Name – Kraken (say it: *krah*-ken)

Type – Underwater monster

Size – When fully grown, about 1.5 miles all round. But sailors have only ever been able to see the whole bodies of young Krakens. Their eggs look like jellyfish.

Habitat – The deep seas of northern Europe

Food – Large sea worms, which it can eat while asleep. It comes to the surface to catch other sea creatures with its tentacles. It may also feed on shipwrecked sailors.

This ancient picture shows a ship anchored to a Kraken. Two sailors have left the ship to cook a meal on the beast's back.

Distinguishing Features

- When awake, the Kraken has huge staring eyes.
- It uses its tentacles to move itself through the water.
- The sea around the Kraken is murky, with a foul smell.

Behaviour

Sailors fear the Kraken, even though it is not aggressive. It stays on the surface for only a short while. When it descends again, the water around it gets stirred up into a whirlpool. Nearby ships and their crews can then be sucked down.

Related Creatures

1. The Kraken is a relative of the squid and the octopus, but it is thousands of times bigger.

2. An even bigger relative is the World Serpent, a monster that circles the whole Earth under the seas. This terrible creature will rise to the surface only at the end of the world.

3. The Zaratan is so big that its back looks like an island, complete with trees, rocks and valleys. But when sailors step onto it, it sinks beneath the waves and drowns them.

Even big fighting ships cannot escape the Kraken's whirlpool.

The Phoenix

The Phoenix is a lonely bird. Only one Phoenix at a time can live in the world – and it lives for 500 years!

This gentle bird's feathers are lovely to see. Its song is lovely to hear. But when it dies, it burns to death. Then it is born again from its own ashes!

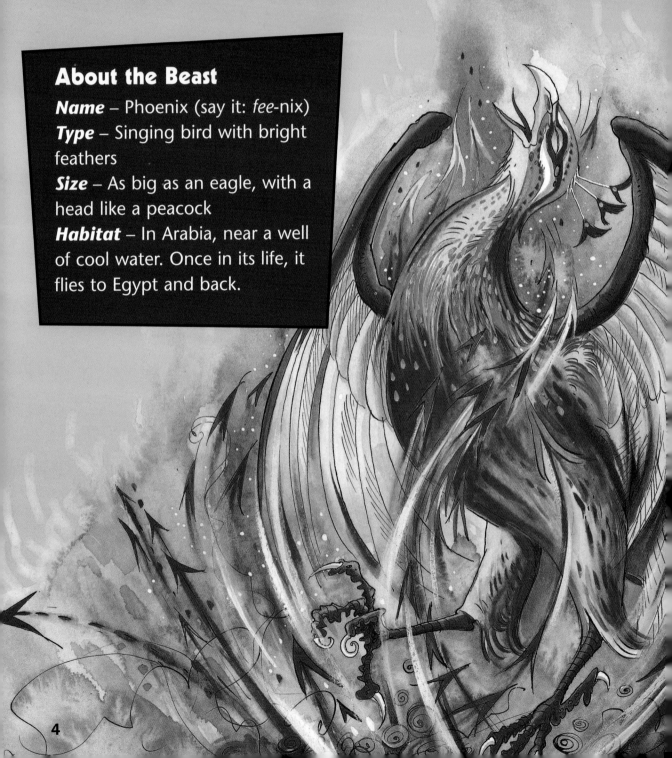

About the Beast

Name – Phoenix (say it: *fee*-nix)

Type – Singing bird with bright feathers

Size – As big as an eagle, with a head like a peacock

Habitat – In Arabia, near a well of cool water. Once in its life, it flies to Egypt and back.

Distinguishing Features

• The feathers of the Phoenix are golden, red and blue.

• Each morning, it washes in the well. Then it sings such a lovely song, the sun stops moving across the sky to listen.

Behaviour

The Phoenix lives for 500 years. Just before it dies, it builds a nest of sweet spices and sits in it. The sun sets the nest on fire, burning the Phoenix up, but a brand new Phoenix springs up from the ashes. It rolls the old bird's ashes into a ball. Then it flies with the ball to the Temple of the Sun in Egypt, and leaves it on the altar.

The Roc

Related Creatures

1. The Roc is a bird that lives in Persia, near Arabia. It also looks like an eagle, but is much bigger than the Phoenix. Its eggs are like great domes. It picks up and eats baby elephants!

2. Avalerion birds live in India. There are only ever two in the world at one time. After sixty years they make two eggs. When the eggs hatch, the parent birds drown themselves.

The Phoenix

The Unicorn

The beautiful Unicorn is a rare and dangerous beast. It moves so fast that people cannot be sure what its body looks like. It has a single long horn with special powers. Hunters chase Unicorns, wanting to break off these horns. Then they aim to use the special powers for themselves.

About the Beast

Name – Unicorn (means 'one horn')

Type – Land animal

Size – A little larger than a horse

Food – It grazes on grass. (The gentle Unicorn of China will not harm any living thing, so it eats only dead grass!)

Habitat – The first Unicorn was seen in India. It is also found in Europe and in Asia – in forests, plains and other wild places.

▲ *The Royal Coat of Arms, with the Lion and the Unicorn working together to support the shield. The nursery rhyme tells a different story:*

The lion and the unicorn
Were fighting for the crown.
The lion beat the unicorn
All around the town.

Behaviour

The Unicorn dips its horn into liquid to see if it is poisonous or not. It can also use its horn to make poisoned water fresh and clean. People carve special cups from the horns of Unicorns. These cups change colour if the drink inside them is poisonous.

The Unicorn runs too fast to be caught by hunters. But if it picks up the scent of a maiden, it will go to her very tamely. Then it falls asleep on her lap. Before it wakes, the young woman can cut off its precious horn.

The Unicorn is beautiful but also fierce. It fights with the lion, and is not afraid of the elephant. Its hoof is so sharp, it can tear an elephant's stomach open with a single kick.

Distinguishing Features

- The Unicorn has the body of a horse, the beard of a goat, and the legs of an antelope.

- In the middle of its forehead it has one long horn. The horn is about half a metre long. It is white at the base, black in the middle and red at the pointed tip.

- People grind down the horns of Unicorns to make powder. This powder can cure diseases. Some say it even brings dead people back to life!

This picture of a lady and a unicorn was woven in France 500 years ago.

Related Creature

The Ki-Lin is a kind of Chinese Unicorn. It looks more like a deer than a horse. Its short horn is made of flesh. This shy, peaceful beast can live for a thousand years. Anybody who sees one has good luck.

Was That a Unicorn?

Few people ever see a Unicorn. But people often think they have. All these beasts have been mistaken for a Unicorn:

1 bull
2 antelope
3 wild ass
4 horse
5 rhinoceros
6 snake!
7 fish!!

A Unicorn making poisoned water fresh and clean ▼

The Dragon

A dragon called Smaug

Most fire-breathing dragons live in or near
water. They can also live deep underground, or
high in the skies. Some of these mighty creatures
are terrible enemies to humans. Others protect people and
their lands. It is not always easy to know which dragons are
good and which are evil!

About the Beast

Name – Dragon (from an old word meaning 'to watch')

Type – Winged reptile

Size – When fully-grown, it can be many times bigger than a crocodile

Habitat – Found all around the world, usually in rivers, lakes, pools and
wells; some Chinese dragons live on rain clouds

Food – Animal or human flesh, cooked by its fiery breath. In summer it
drinks elephant blood, which is especially cool.

Distinguishing Features

- Red, black, white, green or golden in colour
- Skin that is leathery or covered in scales
- Twin horns on head
- Forked tongue
- Sharp fangs and claws
- Large, glaring eyes
- Sometimes wingless – yet still, mysteriously, it can fly!
- Sometimes has a poisonous sting
- Very difficult to kill

Behaviour

- As the old name shows, dragons are there to guard something. It may be a treasure hoard, like Smaug in *The Hobbit*, or the dragon slain by the Old English hero, Beowulf. Or the dragon may be guarding a princess, who needs to be rescued by a brave knight, like St George. Or Shrek!
- Dragons in western lands turn the countryside into desert with their fiery breath. They prey on all that lives there, including people. A western dragon will often build up a great hoard of treasure, then fight to the death to defend it.
- In eastern lands, protecting dragons patrol the skies, rivers and hills. They make sure rain falls so that crops can grow. Their powers come from a tiny pearl in their stomachs.
- Dragons from Ethiopia travel to Arabia in search of food. Five dragons coil around one another to make a kind of boat. Then they cross the sea with their heads out of the water.

Shrek was the film hero who rescued the princess from this dragon.

Related Creatures

1. The Basilisk is a snake with bats' wings and the head of a cock. It has terrifying eyes. Just by looking at most things it can kill them. Even rocks crack apart. Only the weasel can survive. The surest way to kill a Basilisk is to hold a mirror in front of it. When it sees its own reflection, it dies of fright.

2. A great flying serpent lives in Egypt. Every night it spreads darkness over the land. Every morning the sun then chops off its head, to bring back the light. But by evening the serpent is alive again, and again it makes the land dark.

Paolo Uccello's idea of St George and the dragon, painted 500 years ago.

Sweets for Divali

Late in the year, when the clocks go back and the nights are long, Hindus celebrate Divali, the festival of light. Homes are decked with lights, and there are parties and presents. Often the presents are Indian sweets, which are very sweet indeed! Try making these for your next Divali celebrations.

Coconut sweets

(makes about 12)

Ingredients
- 400g tin condensed milk
- 350g grated or desiccated coconut
- 500g icing sugar
- Food colouring
- Icing sugar to decorate

Utensils
- Sieve
- Large bowl
- Wooden spoon
- Tray or large plate
- Knife

Method

1. Sieve the icing sugar into the bowl, stir in the coconut and condensed milk, and mix thoroughly.

2. Divide the mixture into two or three equal-sized portions, and add a different colour to each.

3. Roll or pat each portion flat so that it is about 2cm deep, straighten the edges, and chill overnight in the fridge.

4. Cut into blocks (about 2cm square) or roll into small balls.

5. Lightly sprinkle with icing sugar.

6. Chill again before eating.

Food for Hanukkah

At Hanukkah, Jewish people eat food that has been fried in oil, in memory of the time the *ner tamid* (sacred flame) burned for 8 days without oil in God's honour. Traditional fried foods, such as potato latkes and doughnuts, are often served.

Potato latkes

(makes 10)

Ingredients
- 2 large potatoes
- 2 tbsps plain flour
- 2 eggs
- salt and pepper
- olive oil for frying

Utensils
- potato peeler
- grater
- mixing bowl
- frying pan
- kitchen paper for draining

Method

1. In the bowl, beat the eggs and season with salt and pepper.

2. Peel and grate the potatoes, and drain away any liquid.

3. Add the grated potato and the flour to eggs, and mix thoroughly.

4. Heat the oil in a frying pan, then drop in spoonfuls of the mixture.

5. Fry for a few minutes on each side until golden brown.

6. Drain on kitchen paper and serve immediately.

Celebrating Baisakhi

Baisakhi marks the Sikh New Year's Day in the middle of April, and is a very important festival. In the Punjab (now part of India and Pakistan), Baisakhi is also the time of the harvest, and so sharing food is an important part of any Baisakhi celebrations. 'Karah parshad' is a special food that is shared at the end of prayers.

Karah parshad

You will need
1 cup sugar   1 cup wholemeal flour or semolina
1 cup melted butter   Some water and a little oil

What to do
1. Put the sugar and a little water into a pan. Stir and simmer until the sugar has dissolved.

2. Mix the butter and flour in another pan and fry in a little oil until the flour is golden brown.

3. Add the syrup (sugar water) to the flour and stir over a low heat until the mixture becomes very thick.

4. Leave to cool and set for at least half an hour.

Shrove Tuesday

Christians call the 40 days before Easter 'Lent'. During this time they used to eat very plain food in memory of the 40 days Jesus spent hungry in the desert. So, on the day before Lent began, rich foods, like milk and eggs, were used up. Today, many people still make pancakes on Shrove Tuesday, although not all Christians fast during Lent any longer.

Pancakes
(Serves 2)

Ingredients
- 1 egg
- 200ml milk
- 175ml plain flour
- ½ tbsp oil or a little butter
- 1 tbsp caster sugar
- ½ lemon

Utensils
- Blender
- Medium sized frying pan
- Tablespoon

Method

1. Put the egg and milk into the blender and whizz them up on the highest setting for about 30 seconds (or beat them with a whisk).

2. Turn the blender to low, and gradually pour in the flour. Blend the batter until smooth.

3. Put the batter in the fridge, and leave it to stand for 30 minutes.

4. Heat the oil in the frying pan over a medium heat. Pour in 3 tbsp of the batter and swirl it around the pan.

5. Cook the pancake for about 1 minute, then flip it over and cook the other side.

6. Slide the pancake onto a plate and repeat steps 4 and 5 until you have made 4 pancakes.

7. Sprinkle with lemon and sugar, roll up and serve immediately.

3p

The MORNING CAPER

Thursday 1st April

Issue no. 333

TROLL'S HAD ENOUGH!

Rapping Goats Batter Bridge

Exclusive by Tab Lloyd, **Crime Reporter**

Noisy neighbours are driving a troll right off his trolley! Furious Mr Troll of Under-the-Bridge, By-the-Stream, Pastures Green, is fed up with the constant racket from three goats who insist on galloping over his bridge.

'They sound like a herd of rapping hooligans, trip-trapping all over the place!' the burly Mr Troll told our reporter. 'They're at it twenty-four, seven!'

The goats, all of whom answer to the name of Billy Gruff, refused to be interviewed.

However, the *Caper* understands that Mr Troll plans to eat his neighbours if the trip-trapping doesn't stop. 'I'll have their guts for starters!' he threatened.

Tasty stuff – or just a bluff?

More inside!

P7 Troll-dolls, the grizzly must-have toys

P11 Just Kidding – Great Goat Jokes

P13 No butts! Nanny's topical tips

WHO'S TRIP-TRAPPING OVER MY BRIDGE?

Goats Deny Trip-Trap Trips

*By our Travel Correspondent, **Wanda Farr***

Three Billy Goats Gruff denied today that they were nuisance neighbours. Local bridge owner, Mr Troll, has accused them of trying to drive him from his home by organizing Trip-Trap Trips. He claims that herds of day-trippers now stampede across his private bridge.

'He's talking rot! There's just the three of us,' the Gruffs' spokesman, bearded Big Billy of Next-Door, Round-the-Bend, Butts Bottoms, told our reporter. 'I've never heard of Trip-Trap Trips.' He did admit however, that the Gruffs pop across the bridge from time to time. 'It's the only place to get a decent meal,' he said. 'There's just weed feed around here, but it's class grass over there. Why would we want to share it with other goats?'

To get to the truth, our reporter went undercover and, dressed in a goat costume, attempted to book a bridge crossing with Big Billy. He was at home with his name-sakes, Middle Billy and Little Billy. The Gruffs were lunching on a pile of posters that offered 'Amazing Grazing – Gorgeous Grass for Gobbling Goats'. None of them would comment and they swallowed the evidence. *Suspicious or what?*

The *Caper* understands that Mr Troll has now been seen driving around in a small motor car with sharp blades between the wheels. *Sounds very like a lawnmower to us, Mr Troll!* Watch this space for the latest on the Trip-Trap Case!

Troll's Tactics put an end to Grass Tourism

The People's Pest

3p

Issue No. 1000

Monday, 2nd August, 2004

PIED PIPER CHANGES HIS TUNE

Exclusive, by our Vermin Correspondent, Ro Dent

'Never trust a man in a flashy suit!' was the warning from the Mayor of Hamlyn after today's mass kidnap of the town's children. They were last seen trooping up a mountain following a man wearing a tasteless red and yellow outfit and a silly hat. The kidnapper's description fits that of a wandering minstrel known as the Pied Piper.

Readers may recall our recent coverage of the mass rat migration. Swanky Mr Piper claimed that he was a rodent enchanter and that the rats would toddle when they heard him tootle.

As we know, the Pied Piper did his stuff and the rats skedaddled. But how did he do it? Was it hoodoo or ballyhoo?

A rodent expert believes that the rats may not have

You dirty rat, you! Did he diddle us?

been bewitched by Mr Piper's musical skills. 'They could have been attracted by his gaudy outfit,' he explained. 'It was a bobby-dazzler! Anyone could have put on a silly suit and done the same thing.'

The mayor has now locked himself in the town's safe and was interviewed through the keyhole. 'I knew he was a dodgy dealer!' he said. 'He'll not get a brass farthing!'

The *Pest* understands that when Mr Piper heard that the deal was off, he blew a fuse and threatened revenge. Now our children are missing! *Do we smell a rat? You bet we do!*

PIED PIPER ACCUSED OF RAT RIP-OFF

'I'm No Kidnapper!' says Pop Idol. 'Those Kids were my Fans!'

By our Music Correspondent, **Penny Whistler**

At a press conference today the Pied Piper hit out against allegations that he's a fraud and a kidnapper.

Wearing his trade-mark red and yellow designer gear, the Pied Piper, 21, denied that he'd done anything wrong. 'Like, I can't believe how that Mayor guy didn't recognise me,' he said in his statement. 'He must have heard my album, *Squirmin' Vermin*. It was No. 1 in the Rat Charts like – forever! The guy's ratted on the deal,' he told us. 'I cracked the rat pack, so I should get the cash. I mean, that's cool isn't it?

Hey, he got a good deal. He was paying me big bucks so I threw in a gig for free – yeah, for free! Hey man, the guy had something to celebrate. So why not party?'

When asked about the kidnapping, PP denied knowing anything. 'Chill out, guys,' he told us. 'I'm no kidnapper. Those kids are my fans! They were just queuing up for the gig.'

When asked why the children hadn't returned home, PP was reluctant to comment further. 'Hey, get real,' he told us. 'I got rid of the rats. So, where's the dosh, Tosh? Kids for

quids! Get my drift? OK, you guys?'

Oh, yes, PP, we get your drift. Oh no, PP, it's not OK! Where are our children? The Pest will investigate. The Pest Quest begins here!

THE ROMAN SOLDIER

The Roman Army

The Roman Empire was carved out and defended by the Roman army – an effective and disciplined army, whose reputation has stood the test of time. The soldiers were brave and strong and worked well together. What kinds of things was a Roman soldier asked to do? What was his life like?

Training

The Roman infantry were trained to obey orders and to help their comrades. The training was tough, and the soldiers' fitness was famous. New recruits built up their strength with twice-daily marching drill (practice) and 18-mile cross-country marches three times a month. They did weapons-training with swords and javelins and learned to defend themselves with shields. The training weapons were extra heavy, so that the real ones would be easy to handle in battle.

A soldier had to be very strong. As well as carrying his armour and weapons, each soldier marched with his kit in leather bags slung from a pole. The bags held his bedding, spare clothes, food dish, cooking pot and rations for three days. He also carried his tools: pick, saw, axe, billhook, basket and a length of chain.

Soldiers on a Roman carving

Here are sample pages from history books and a magazine.

A soldier's gear

Javelin: *over two metres long, with a wooden handle and a metal tip*

Sword: *about 50cm long and 5cm wide, worn in a sheath on the right side*

Tunic: *thigh-length, coarse wool. Later on, soldiers wore short trousers instead*

Equipment: *included tools, weapons and cooking pot, as well as blankets and bedding*

Helmet: *made of iron to protect head, face and neck*

Metal jacket: *metal strips held together by leather straps. It was so heavy soldiers had to help each other put it on*

Belt: *the sheath was attached to the belt, and a protective apron of leather, reinforced with metal, hung down in front*

Shield: *wood with a metal stud in the centre to strengthen it. It was 1.6m tall*

Sandals: *leather, fastened with leather thongs. The soles were reinforced with iron studs to make them strong enough for marching*

A soldier's life

The soldiers did not spend their whole time fighting. Once an area had been conquered, there were fortifications to build, roads to make, and special tasks like the building of Hadrian's Wall (across the north of England), which was carried out by the army. There was also weapons-training, and equipment to make and to mend.

Wallsend

Segudunum was the fort at Wallsend, at the eastern end of Hadrian's Wall. It had a stone rampart with four gateways and 10 watchtowers. Soldiers lived in the barracks. How did a soldier spend his day when he wasn't out fighting? **Gaius Fulvius recounts a typical day:**

- Up at sunrise. It's cold here in winter, so we have extra blankets and a fire.

- Breakfast – just beer and porridge as usual.

- Roll call. Kit inspection. Extra issue of trousers and socks. Snow's on the way. Will I ever get used to it?

- After roll call, Training. Today we're practising setting up a temporary camp.

- After training, Duties. My mates are off to the quarry to hack out more stone for the wall, but I'm a leather worker, so I'll be working on the new issue of soldiers' shoes.

- Duty done, I have some free time. I've got a pass, so I'm off to see Bronac and the baby!

- Evening mess. We're meant to cook our own food, but in my unit we take turns. My turn tonight. I'm cooking a stew and I've managed to get hold of a ration of figs for a treat.

- Sundown – back to barracks. The nights are long, but we're tired after all the heavy work. Besides, Marcus is telling us a story about home. We lie and listen and pretend we're back in Gaul again.

Did Gaius Fulvius look like this?

QUEEN VICTORIA

A Long Reign

Victoria ruled the United Kingdom for 64 years – longer than any other British monarch. She became queen in 1837, and reigned until she died in 1901. She was the first Queen for over a century, and lived at a time when women stayed in the background, so she really stood out. She wrote masses of letters to her ministers and to her family, and kept a diary from the age of 8, so we have an inside view of her life.

Family Matters

Victoria was born into the British royal family in 1819. Her parents were the Duke of Kent and Victoria, a German princess. In 1837, at the age of 18, she was made queen. This was because she was the nearest royal relative to King William IV, who had just died. She married her German cousin, Prince Albert, and despite once calling babies 'nasty objects' she had nine children with him! When she died she left 31 grandchildren.

Someone To Look Up To

Victoria became a mother-figure for the British people, and also for the people of Britain's worldwide Empire. This stretched from Canada in the west, through India and South Africa to Australia and the Far East. In 1876 she took the title Empress of India, and from then on she always signed her name Victoria RI (short for Queen and Empress in Latin). There were huge parties called 'jubilees' to mark 50 years of her rule in 1887, then 60 years in 1897. British people came to look up to Victoria – even though she was barely 5 feet tall!

Contents

Victorian Times

Victoria was an ordinary woman, who ruled at a busy, exciting time in British history. One big change in her century was that more people were allowed to vote. This meant that they could elect Members of Parliament to speak up for them. The problem was that quite a lot of people could not read and write. It was hard for them to find out the truth about things. The Government built schools and passed laws to make parents send their children along, so that they could be educated.

Going with the Flow

Another big change was the railway network. The Queen and Albert had a royal railway carriage fitted out. In it they rode all over Britain on the network of new railways. They especially loved going to Scotland, where they had holidays at Balmoral Castle. She was also fascinated by another British invention – photography – and had many photos taken of her growing family.

Victoria and Albert and their nine children

The Great Exhibition

The Great Exhibition of 1851 displayed the very latest products of modern science and technology. It took place in central London in a beautiful glass building called the Crystal Palace. The Exhibition was tremendously popular. Six million tickets were sold. Many people came from other parts of the country on special trains. Queen Victoria herself visited it 34 times!

When it was all over, the profits were used to build magnificent museums and concert halls, like the Science Museum and the Royal Albert Hall. Queen Victoria called it 'the triumph of my beloved Albert' because it was his vision and energy that carried the project through. It is sad that he did not live to see his grand design completed. He caught typhoid and died in 1861. The grief-stricken queen wore black for the rest of her life.

Victoria with her beloved Prince Albert. 'There is no one to call me Victoria now,' she wrote when he died.

Unequal Opportunities

Victoria lived in royal luxury, but for most British people life was hard. Many soldiers died in wars like the Crimean War against Russia (1853–56), and the Boer War in Africa (1899–1902). In Britain's big factory cities, there were epidemics of cholera and typhoid. Crime spread too, and the newly formed police force did its best to contain it. In Ireland a terrible famine began in 1845. People left the country in droves, and went to America, Africa and Australia. The government tried to solve some of these problems, but big changes were needed to give everyone in Victoria's Britain a fairer chance in life.

So You Want to Know about
Michael Owen?

Michael Owen is the youngest footballer to play for England since the 1800s. Before he was 23, he had played in two World Cups. Before 24, he captained his country. He scored in his first game as skipper. Although he is only 1.76m tall (5' 7"), he is easily the biggest star now playing in England.

Schoolboy Star

Michael showed huge talent from a very early age. Born in Chester in 1979, he was the fourth of five children, and took up football when he was 7. His speed and skill soon made him the top striker in the Deeside Primary Schools League. By the time he was 11, all England's big professional clubs had heard of him.

On the Road to Glory

Michael had only one dream now: to be a professional footballer. He joined the Football Association's School of Excellence at Lilleshall. He studied hard there, passing his GCSEs as well as playing for England's Under-15, Under-16 and Under-17 teams. In his first game for each team, he scored! Meanwhile he helped Liverpool win the FA Youth Cup. Then in 1996, when he turned 17, his dream came true: Liverpool signed him as a professional player.

In 1998 Michael was voted BBC TV's Sports Personality of the Year. He was still only 18 years old.

Man at the Top

Michael soon broke into the Liverpool first team. He never looked back. In 1997 he scored in his first game. For the next five seasons he was Liverpool's top goal-scorer – helping the club win three major cups. Meanwhile, at the age of 18, he joined David Beckham and Co. in the England squad for the 1998 World Cup. England were knocked out on penalties by Argentina, but earlier in the game Michael scored one of the best goals ever seen. That goal made him a hero to football fans right around the world.

Michael's wonder goal for England against Argentina at the 1998 World Cup. After receiving a pass from David Beckham, Michael sped through the Argentina defence then blazed the ball past goalkeeper Carlos Roa.

Keeping it in the Family

Success has changed many young football stars – but not Michael. Despite his fame and wealth, he still likes having his family around. He even bought houses in the same street for himself and his closest relatives! Some media reporters call him 'Mr Goody Twoshoes' and try to catch him misbehaving in his free time. But Michael has no interest in clubbing or nightlife. The clubs he likes are golf clubs! The nightlife he enjoys is playing football under floodlights!

GLORIOUS GOAL STATISTICS
Michael Owen in the Premiership:

Season	Games	Goals
1996-7	2	1
1997-8	36	18
1998-9	30	18
1999-2000	27	11
2000-1	28	16
2001-2	29	19
2002-3	35	19

Michael Owen for England:
International Games Played 50
Goals Scored 22

COVERS AND CONTENTS

You can learn a lot from the cover of a book.

WHY do volcanoes erupt?

Questions children ask

?? Heinemann InfoSearch

Why do Bruises Change Colour?

· and other questions about blood ·

Angela Royston

Get Writing!

Get Writing last scene

Write that Film Script

Shaun McCarthy

BINES · BRIDGES · JETS · OIL RIGS · TELEPHONES · DAM

HOW THINGS WORK

FASCINATING PROJECTS AND EXPERIMENTS THAT REVEAL THE SECRETS OF TECHNOLOGY

NEIL ARDLEY

COMPUTER MEMORY · ROCKETS · SKYSCRAPERS · GEARS

HERS · WASHING MACHINES · AQUALUNGS

The contents page explains what is to be found in the book.
This one is taken from 'Life in Space' by David Glover.

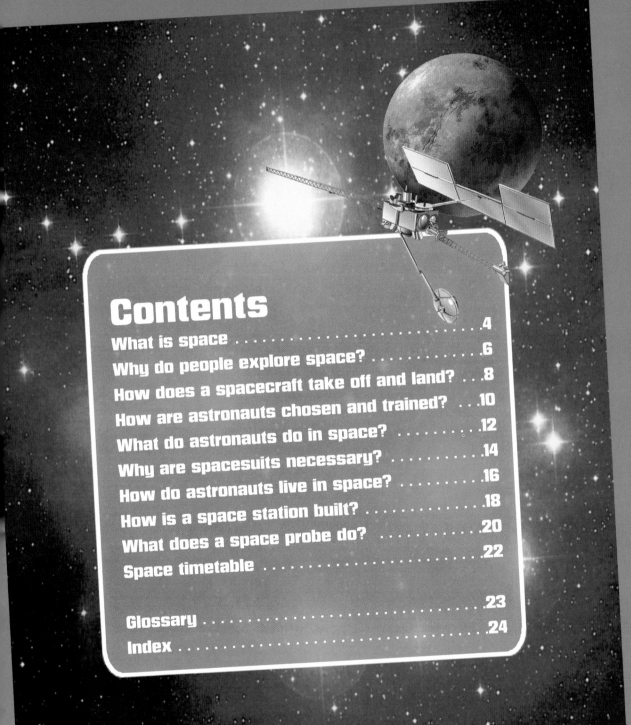

Contents

How does a SPACECRAFT take off and land?

Astronauts travel into space inside a spacecraft made up of a capsule powered by rockets. The rocket engines burn fuel, which produces hot gases.

Taking off

When the spacecraft is ready to take off, the hot gases shoot out from the engines and push the rocket up from the ground. The force must be big enough to overcome the Earth's gravity.

The main rocket may be helped away from the launch pad by booster rockets fixed to its sides. When the rocket is going fast enough, the boosters fall away.

Staying in orbit

The rocket engines turn off when the spacecraft reaches orbit. It does not need engines to keep going in space because there is no air. This means there is no friction so the spacecraft does not slow down.

Landing

When the astronauts want to return to Earth they turn on the engines, to push their spacecraft out of orbit. Gravity then pulls the spacecraft back towards the Earth. The spacecraft may be slowed to a safe landing speed by parachutes. The space shuttle has stubby wings so that it can land on a runway like an aeroplane, but many spacecraft splash down gently into the sea.

❶ command module with three astronauts

❷ engines

❸ booster rockets

❹ hot gases

❺ launch pad

A Russian SL-4 taking off. During take off, the astronauts are strapped into seats inside a capsule on top of the rocket. There is not much for them to do, as the take off is controlled by a computer.

Look at these adverts. The text has been taken away.

Who do you think they are aimed at?
What are they trying to sell?

Some ads rely on clever wordplay.
What do you think of these?

NEVER EAT A **Munch bar** WHILST MASQUERADING AS A MATADOR IN MADRID.

...hen eating - especially if you're wearing red.

Little Miss Muffet sat on a tuffet
eating her curds and whey.
There came a big spider,
who sat down beside her,
which she immediately identified
as Tegenaria gigantea.

'CREEPY-CRAWLIES' AT THE NATURAL HISTORY MUSEUM. YOU CAN ALWAYS SPOT A KID WHO'S BEEN
http://www.nhm.ac.uk

THE NATURAL HISTORY MUSEUM

34

WINTER SKILLS FOR SCOTTISH HILLS!

Special Offer: £20 off all winter Holidays!

We offer a range of great value winter skills and mountaincraft courses based at Cairngorm Lodge, Braemar and Crianlarich Youth Hostels.

All of our holidays are led by fully-qualified leaders and offer expert tuition at a price you can afford.

Winter SKILLS WEEKENDS · Winter mountaincraft Winter HILLS and munros

For more information visit www.HostelHolidays.com or call 0870 1 55 32 55 for your free brochure.

Our promises to our customers.

1 Treat your vehicle with care and always fit protective seat covers.

2 Ensure your vehicle is inspected by a technically qualified staff member.

3 Examine the vehicle with you and give an honest appraisal of the work required.

4 Give you a binding quotation which includes all associated charges prior to work commencing.

5 Ensure you are aware that any non exchange part or component removed from your vehicle is available for you to take away.

6 Ensure that all work is carried out in accordance with the company's laid down procedures.

7 Inform you immediately of any complications or delays.

8 Ensure that all completed work is checked by a technically qualified staff member.

9 Offer to inspect the finished work with you at the time of delivery.

TV – SWITCH ON OR SWITCH OFF?

Television is very popular. Almost every home in the UK has at least one TV set. But did you know that children in the UK watch more television than children in any other country in Europe? Should we be worried by this? Or is watching TV just good harmless fun?

Switch on!

Many parents assert that television is good for their children. It entertains and relaxes them. But more importantly, they believe their children can learn a lot from the programmes they watch. It's true that children seem to like programmes that educate and inform them. In fact, the most popular children's programme of 2002 was *Newsround*. Parents have also noticed that their children still enjoy other activities, besides TV, such as reading and sport.

In addition, many parents are happy to let their children watch what they like on TV. This is because they trust the rules about what can be shown on UK television. For example, there is a rule that all news programmes must be accurate and impartial. Another rule requires programmes broadcast before 9 p.m. to be suitable for family viewing. So most parents feel it is safe to let children have TV sets in their bedrooms.

Three quarters of children between 5 and 16 years old have TVs in their bedrooms.

- *Half of the twelve most popular children's programmes in 2002 were factual programmes.*
- *Even though there is now more children's television than ever, TV has not affected the numbers of children who read for pleasure.*
- *Programmes shown in the UK must not contain anything that the general public would find offensive.*
- *All programmes between 5.30 a.m. and 9 p.m. must be suitable for family viewing.*

and everyone can follow the arguments.
Here are a few examples of ways to do it.

Switch off!

On the other hand, there are parents who feel their children should watch less TV. They are worried by the fact that, every year, children are becoming fatter and less active. They put this down to the amount of time spent sitting in front of the small screen. They also think that letting children have their own televisions and giving them access to satellite and cable TV means they will watch it more than ever!

These parents are also worried about the sorts of programmes their children watch. For example, they think that programmes, like *EastEnders* and *The Bill*, have unsuitable storylines and show too much violence for children. They would like TV programmes to be given an age certificate, in the same way as films are. They believe that children's programmes on cable and satellite are not as educational as ones on BBC and ITV.

- *The most popular TV programmes watched by children in 2002 were adult programmes. EastEnders was their favourite.*
- *Children who have TVs in their bedrooms get less sleep than children who do not.*
- *Children who have satellite and digital TV watch more TV than children who don't.*
- *There is now often more violence on TV before nine o'clock than after it!*

So who is right? Do children need to switch off that TV set and do other things? Or is watching television a good way for children to spend their free time? Should parents worry about which programmes their children see? Or is most television suitable for children to watch? What do you think?

WHO'D BE A TEACHER?

Would you like your teacher's job? Is teaching your idea of a terrific job or a terrible job? Here some Year 4 children give their views.

Just the job!

• **Teaching has to be the best job ever! Just think of all those long holidays and short working days.**

• *It must be very rewarding being a teacher. You can help so many children to learn to read and write.*

• **I reckon the best thing about being a teacher is being able to boss people about! Imagine all that power! I'd love to be in charge for once.**

• I love reading and maths and art. It must be amazing to be able to teach all your favourite subjects.

• **Teachers are lucky. They get lots of presents from their pupils at Christmas and they don't have to wear uniform! And they get to eat biscuits at break times. How lucky is that!**

• *I think teaching must be a really important job. If you do your job properly your class will do well. It must be a great feeling if you get this right.*

Children respect teachers who listen to them and encourage them.

• *Experienced teachers can earn over £30,000 a year.*

• *Teachers have 12 weeks holiday a year.*

• *Children like teachers who help them and who manage to make them feel clever.*

• *Teachers must work 195 days a year plus any other hours that are necessary.*

40

You must be joking!

• I wouldn't want to be a teacher. They have to work hard at college and pass lots of exams. And then they still have to do more training when they are a teacher!

• **People say teachers have long holidays. But my dad is a teacher and he spends most of his weekends and holidays doing school work.**

• I think teaching must be a very hard job. It must be horrible when children ruin your lessons by messing around.

• My uncle has just started teaching. He says he spends more time doing paperwork than teaching!

• There aren't enough teachers because people don't want to do the job. It said so on the news. It's because teachers have too much work.

• *I think teaching is very stressful. If your children don't do well in tests, everyone thinks it's your fault!*

Many teachers find that their workload interferes with their home life.

> • **Teachers work over 52 hours a week during term time.**
>
> • **Many class teachers work another 113 hours during the school holidays.**
>
> • **Long hours and overwork are the main reasons why people leave teaching or don't want to become teachers.**

So what do you think?
Would you want to be a teacher?
Does it sound just the job for you or the last thing you would do?

SCHOOL UNIFORM

Dress to impress!

Wear uniform and show pride in your school and your appearance.

- *Avoid wasting time in the morning deciding what to wear!*

- *Save money on expensive new clothes.*

- *Avoid the pressure of keeping up with the latest fashions.*

- *Cut the risk of being bullied for what you wear.*

Wear Uniform – It's the Cool School Rule!

GREAT OR GROSS?

Stand Out from the Crowd

WEAR WHAT YOU WANT NOT WHAT SCHOOL WANTS!

- *Avoid the boredom of wearing the same clothes every day!*

- *Be free to wear the styles and colours that suit you.*

- *Save money by not buying expensive uniform.*

- *Avoid the embarrassment of wearing dull and dated clothes!*

Dare to be Different!

NOTICE

PROPOSED NEW DINING ARRANGEMENTS

A proposal has been put forward by Max Snax Ltd, a local catering company.

The company is proposing to:
- Provide a new menu for school children, teachers and other adults at the school. This will include burgers, a range of other meals, drinks and snacks;
- Cook the meals on the premises every day;
- Train and employ local people to help cook and serve the meals;
- Update and expand the existing eating areas within the school.

The proposal is currently being considered by the Local Education Authority and the school governors. As you will know, I am in favour of the proposal. However, not everyone agrees that this will solve our long-running school dinner problems. I am therefore inviting everyone involved in the school – teaching and other staff, parents and pupils – to visit the exhibition in the school hall on Thursday 16th June, and to take part in the public meeting on the same evening at 7.30.

Signed: *Robert McNamee*   Headteacher

Dear Mr Greenberg,

I am glad to hear you have decided to send David to us. I'm sure you will not regret your decision.

You had a question about the catering arrangements for school dinners. I'm sorry to say that these have been put on hold since the fire in the canteen. Children are bringing packed lunches, which they eat outside when it is fine, and in the school hall when it rains. More permanent arrangements are under discussion, and we are hoping these will be completed over the summer holidays. All will be in place when David arrives among us in September…

Menu

hot food
chicken nuggets (8 pieces)
beef burger
veggie burger
beef burger with cheese

99p
99p
99p
£1.10p

side dishes
regular chips
small chips
baked beans
hash browns
peas
side salad

60p
50p
35p
35p
35p
50p

sauces
tomato, barbecue, mayonnaise   FREE

cold food
cheese roll
sandwiches
sausage roll
range of crisps

80p
80p
90p
20p

puddings
apple Danish
cinnamon Danish
individual apple pie

60p
60p
60p

drinks
fruit juice
cans of pop
orangeade or lemonade

50p
50p
30p

Artist's impression of the proposed dining arrangements

It's great eating outside. We always eat our packed lunch in the tree house.

My mum says there's no goodness in processed food.

Your mum wants the school to cook its own meals and keep chickens on the scraps.

Cool! I'll look after the chickens!

Did you hear about the burger bar? It'll be like having lunch at McDonald's every day!

WOW!

INDEX